THE RIGHT TO
LEAD

LEARNING LEADERSHIP THROUGH
CHARACTER AND COURAGE

JOHN C. MAXWELL

THOMAS NELSON
Since 1798

NASHVILLE DALLAS MEXICO CITY RIO DE JANEIRO

TABLE OF CONTENTS

MARE BALEARIDES

INSULÆ

Ins. MINORCA

S. Bajoli
S. Catherine

Fornello
Port Fornello

Citadella

Alior

Puglionza

MALIOR-

Maon
Port de Maon

Soter

CA Mallorca

Alcudia

C. de la Phra

Laire de Maon

Dragonera

Palomora
Porto

Catalonga

Porto Colombo

Cap
Figuer
Porto Pedro

BALE. INS.

ARICUM

c. de Tupomago

Cabrera Ins.

PYTYUSÆ

NSULÆ

mentora I.
ra el
nsa

I
T
E
R
R
A
N
E
I

I
T
E
R
R
A
N

I. de

Sargel

What Gives a Man or Woman the Right to Lead?

It certainly isn't gained by election or appointment. Having position, title, rank, or degrees doesn't qualify anyone to lead other people. And the ability doesn't come automatically from age or experience, either.

No, it would be accurate to say that no one can be given the right to lead. The right to lead can only be earned. And that takes time.

The Kind of Leader Others Want to Follow

The key to becoming an effective leader is not to focus on making other people follow, but on making yourself the kind of person they want to follow. You must become someone others can trust to take them where they want to go.

As you prepare yourself to become a better leader, use the following guidelines to help you grow:

1) Let go of your ego.

The truly great leaders are not in leadership for personal gain. They lead in order to serve other people. Perhaps that is why Lawrence D. Bell remarked, "Show me a man who cannot bother to do little things, and I'll show you a man who cannot be trusted to do big things."

2) Become a good follower first.

Rare is the effective leader who didn't learn to become a good follower first. That is why a leadership institution such as the United States Military Academy teaches its officers to become effective followers first—and why West Point has produced more leaders than the Harvard Business School.

3) Build positive relationships.

Leadership is influence, nothing more, nothing less. That means it is by nature relational. Today's generation of leaders seem particularly aware of this because title and position mean so little to them. They know intuitively that people go along with people they get along with.

4) Work with excellence.

No one respects and follows mediocrity. Leaders who earn the right to lead give their all to what they do. They bring into play not only their skills and talents, but also great passion and hard work. They perform on the highest level of which they are capable.

5) Rely on discipline, not emotion.

Leadership is often easy during the good times. It's when everything seems to be against you—when you're out of energy, and you don't want to lead—that you earn your place as a leader. During every season of life, leaders face crucial moments when they must choose between gearing up or giving up. To make it through those times, rely on the rock of discipline, not the shifting sand of emotion.

6) Make adding value your goal.

When you look at the leaders whose names are revered long after they have finished leading, you find that they were men and women who helped people to live better lives and reach their potential. That is the highest calling of leadership—and its highest value.

7) Give your power away.

One of the ironies of leadership is that you become a better leader by sharing whatever power you have, not by saving it all for yourself. You're meant to be a river, not a reservoir. If you use your power to empower others, your leadership will extend far beyond your grasp.

❖ ❖ ❖

In *The Right to Lead,* you will hear from and read about people who have done these same things and earned the right to lead others. Because of the courage they found and the character they displayed, other people recognized their admirable qualities and felt compelled to follow them.

The followers who looked to these leaders learned from them, and so can we. As you explore their worlds and words, remember that it takes time to become worthy of followers. Leadership isn't learned or earned in a moment.

John C. Maxwell

SECTION ONE

ACTION

❖

Men are alike in their promises.

It is only in their deeds that they differ.

—MOLIÉRE

11

DOING
WHAT'S RIGHT
EARNS
YOU THE RIGHT

When U.S. Army General H. Norman Schwarzkopf was a colonel stationed in Vietnam, he commanded the First Battalion of the Sixth Infantry, a unit previously known as the "worst of the sixth" but which he turned around with strong leadership.

After he improved the battalion, it was reassigned to a place Schwarzkopf described as "a horrible, malignant place" called the Batangan Peninsula. It was an area that had been fought over for thirty years, was covered with mines and booby traps, and was the site of numerous weekly casualties from those devices.

Schwarzkopf made the best of a bad situation. He introduced procedures to greatly reduce casualties, and whenever a soldier was injured by a mine, he flew out to check on the man, evacuated him using his personal chopper, and talked to the other men to boost their morale.

On May 28, 1970, a man was injured by a mine, and Schwarzkopf flew to where he lay. While his helicopter was evacuating the soldier, another man stepped on a mine, severely injuring his leg. The man thrashed around on the ground, screaming and wailing. That's when everyone realized the first mine hadn't been a lone booby trap. They were in fact standing in the middle of a minefield.

Schwarzkopf believed the injured man could survive, and even keep his leg—but only if he stopped flailing around. There was only one thing Schwarzkopf could do. He had to go after the man and immobilize him. In his autobiography, *It Doesn't Take a Hero*, Schwarzkopf wrote:

I started through the minefield, one slow step at a time, staring at the ground, looking for telltale bumps or little prongs sticking up from the dirt. My knees were shaking so hard that each time I took a step, I had to grab my leg and steady it with both hands before I could take another. . . . It seemed like a thousand years before I reached the kid.[1]

The 240-pound Schwarzkopf, who had been a wrestler at West Point, then pinned the wounded man and calmed him down. It saved the man's life. And eventually with the help of an engineer team, Schwarzkopf was able to get him and the others out of the minefield.

Later that night when Schwarzkopf was at the hospital, three black soldiers stopped him in a hallway and said, "Colonel, we saw what you did for the brother out there. We'll never forget that, and we'll make sure that all the other brothers in the battalion know what you did." Until that moment, it hadn't occurred to him that the soldier he had saved was black.

The army had given Schwarzkopf the power to lead. And his knowledge and skill had given him the ability to lead. But his demonstrated character and courage under the most difficult of circumstances had earned him the right to lead.

The basis of courage is individual initiative.
If we cannot act alone, we cannot act together.

—JOHN C. MAXWELL

Resolved:
never to do anything which I should
be afraid to do if it were the last hour
of my life.

—JONATHAN EDWARDS

I submit to you that leaders will never be more or less than their soldier's evaluation of them. This is the true efficiency report. From most of your troops you can expect courage to match your courage, guts to match your guts, endurance to match your endurance, motivation to match your motivation, esprit to match your esprit, a desire for achievement to match your desire for achievement. You can expect a love of God, a love of country, and a love of duty. They won't mind the heat if you sweat with them, and they won't mind the cold if you shiver with them.

You see, you don't accept the troops; they were there first. They accept you. And when they do, you'll know. They won't beat drums, wave flags, or carry you off the drill field on their shoulders, but you'll know. You see, your orders will appoint you to command. No orders, letters, no insignia of rank can appoint you as a leader. Leadership is an intangible thing. Leadership is developed within yourselves, and you'll get stronger as you go.

—*Author Unknown*

LEADER
OF THE PACK

A good student of leadership can learn lessons almost anywhere. Recently I received this letter from a friend who discovered what it takes to lead up near the top of the world:

Dear John,

In August 1999, my wife, Minnietta, and I vacationed with some friends who live in a remote part of Alaska near Denali Park. One day they took us to visit their neighbor, Jeff King, who lives a few miles away. Jeff is a sled-dog racer who has won the 1,000-mile Iditarod race from Anchorage to Nome, Alaska, three times (1993, 1996, and 1998). It was a joy to experience Jeff's love and passion for his seventy huskies and his admiration for their maturity, strength, and courage.

Jeff told us that when he starts the Iditarod race, he starts with sixteen dogs and rotates the lead dog frequently to give all the dogs a chance to lead since every one of them wants to be the lead dog. Eventually, he finds the dog that is the real leader because it is a dog that is energetic and persistent in leading, and that dog becomes the leader of the pack. It is chosen as the leader because it leads; it is able to motivate the other dogs to follow by its own energy and enthusiasm.

Jeff told us that in 1996, the lead dog was a two-and-a-half-year-old female named Jenna. That was very unusual since there were only two females in the pack, she was so young, and she was smaller than all the male dogs. But Jeff said with emotion, "She was our leader; when a blizzard came, she didn't give up. She kept barking and running even when the snow was over her head and inspired us all to keep going. Even at her young age, she has the mental maturity of a leader." When Jeff was congratulated for winning the 1998 Iditarod, he lifted up his lead dog and said, "Here is the leader who won the race for us."

John, I found this story very inspiring and hope you might be able to use it. Grace and peace.

Sincerely,
Kent Millard[2]

Leadership is important no matter who you are or where you lead. And even in a pack of dogs, the one who stays in front has to earn the right to lead.

Character can.

—JOHN C. MAXWELL

You will never do anything worthwhile
in this world without courage.

—JAMES ALLEN

He who loses wealth loses much;
he who loses a friend loses more;
but he that loses courage loses all.

—MIGUEL DE CERVANTES

Uncommon Leaders

Men and women who lead on the highest level are quite extraordinary. They are people of action who have their priorities in line. I've found that there are some common threads in these uncommon leaders.

They are:

Futurists:
Their dreams are bigger than their memories.

Lobbyists:
Their cause outlives and outspeaks their critics.

Catalysts:
They initiate movement and momentum for others.

Specialists:
They don't do everything; they do one thing well.

Optimists:
They believe in their cause and their people beyond reason.

Economists:
They value every resource as a steward of their cause.

Activists:
They are doers and empower others by their actions.

Strategists:
They plan how to use every resource available to be successful.

Enthusiasts:
They have a passion that defies logic and magnetically attracts others.

Pragmatists:
Their legacy is that they solve the practical problems people face.

Industrialists:
They roll up their sleeves and work hard.

Finalists:
They labor with diligence and dedication to the end so that they finish well.

Most of the significant things done
in the world were done by persons
who were either too busy or too sick!
There are few ideal and leisurely settings
for the disciplines of growth.

—ROBERT THORNTON HENDERSON

*Courage teaches us what should be feared
and what ought not to be feared. Only by
taking action do we gain that knowledge.
And from that knowledge comes
an inner strength that inspires us to persevere in
the face of great adversity—and inspires others
to follow. In the most difficult of times,
courage is what makes someone a leader.*

—JOHN C. MAXWELL

SECTION TWO

VISION

❖

The very essence of leadership is you have a vision. It's got to be a vision you articulate clearly and forcefully on every occasion. You can't blow an uncertain trumpet.

—Theodore Hesburgh

Learning Leadership Through Character and Courage

FREE AT LAST

The day that Nelson Mandela was finally to be freed from a South African prison, he got a little restless. He was scheduled to be released at 3:00 in the afternoon, and the process was running behind schedule. He didn't want his people to be disappointed after having waited to see him for so long.

As he and his wife, Winnie, approached the gates around 4:00 p.m., Mandela expected to see several dozen people, mostly family and friends. But as he got closer, he saw a great commotion. He realized there was a huge throng of people— hundreds of reporters, photographers, and television journalists, as well as over a thousand well-wishers. In his autobiography, *Long Walk to Freedom*, he remarked:

Within twenty feet or so of the gate, the cameras started clicking, a noise that sounded like some great heard of metallic beasts. Reporters started shouting questions; television crews began crowding in; ANC [African National Congress] supporters were yelling and cheering. It was a happy, if slightly disorienting chaos.[3]

Mandela's freedom was a long time coming, and he had gained it because of his incredible leadership.

From Driver of Cattle to Leader of People

When Rolihlahla "Nelson" Mandela was born in 1918, his family expected him to make his living herding cattle, as they did. But when he was twelve, his father died, and Mandela became the ward of Chief David Dalindyebo, Paramount Chief of his tribe, the Thembu people. It was under the influence of Dalindyebo that Nelson first became aware of leadership. His guardian often presided over days-long tribal meetings and was always able to lead the people to consensus.

Observing his guardian as a leader in action was only part of what spurred Mandela to achieve. In 1964 he wrote of his childhood:

> My political interest was first aroused when I listened to the elders of our tribe in my village as a youth. They spoke of the good old days before the arrival of the White man. Our people lived peacefully under the democratic rule of their kings and counselors. . . . The elders would tell us about the liberation and how it was fought by our ancestors in defense of our country, as well as the acts of valour performed by generals and soldiers during those epic days. I hoped, and vowed then, that amongst the pleasures that life might offer me would be the opportunity to serve my people and make my own humble contribution to their struggle for freedom.[4]

That desire to serve prompted him to enter the legal profession after graduating from the University of South Africa. He wanted to become a change agent, and law seemed like the best course of action.

In the early 1940s, Mandela joined the ANC. He and a group of associates were determined to create a massive movement to change the way blacks were treated in his country. In the mid 1940s, he and some others formed the African National Congress Youth League (ANCYL) to help accelerate that process. It didn't take long for his fellow members to recognize his leadership and strength, and in 1947, he was elected to its secretaryship.

During the 1950s, Mandela and his associates worked hard to create change in their country, calling for mass strikes, boycotts, protests, and passive resistance. But their efforts met with little success. Meanwhile, the government's oppression of non-whites increased, taking away more of their rights. When Mandela and 150 others were indicted for treason in 1956, the future of the cause looked dark. Mandela fought the charges in court for six years and was finally acquitted. But he knew the Apartheid government would not leave him alone, so he went into hiding. Often he would disguise himself as a chauffeur or common laborer. He was dubbed the Black Pimpernel.

Life As a Prisoner

When Mandela surfaced, he was quickly arrested, tried, and sentenced to five years in prison. During that trial, Mandela said:

> *During my lifetime I have dedicated myself to the struggle of the African people. I have fought against white domination, and I have fought against black domination. I have cherished the ideal of a democratic and free society in which all persons live together in harmony and with equal opportunities. It is an ideal which I hope to live for and to achieve. But if needs be, it is an ideal for which I am prepared to die.[5]*

Once Mandela was in prison, he and other ANC leaders were charged with another crime. This time he was accused of sabotage. He and his colleagues were convicted and sentenced to life in prison.

For over twenty years, Mandela led his people subtly and covertly from prison. Twice leaders in the government tried to bribe him by offering him freedom in exchange for the denunciation of his convictions. The first time, he was told he could leave prison if he would support the government's policy to relocate its black inhabitants. The second time, he was told he could go free if he would renounce violence. Both times he refused. Finally in 1986, as the world showered its disapproval on the Apartheid government, and resistance from blacks in South Africa continually increased, the government initiated secret talks with Mandela. Those discussions eventually led to the dismantling of the Apartheid government and Mandela's release on February 11, 1990.

Unthinkable!

On May 10, 1994, people around the world celebrated when they heard the news that Nelson Mandela had been inaugurated as the president of South Africa. What had been unthinkable only a decade before had come to pass. A black man was president of a country that had been the strongest symbol of racial oppression on the globe.

Mandela was then seventy-five years old. He had spent his whole life fighting for this—the vision his tribal elders had instilled in him as a boy. He was helping to create a nation where the people would have a chance to live peacefully under democratic rule. And he was the only one in the world who could do it. He had earned the right to lead the nation of South Africa.

A leader knows the way,
goes the way, and shows the way.

—JOHN C. MAXWELL

❖ ❖ ❖

A VISION WITH HEART

Leadership always requires courage. In fact, the word courage comes from the French word coeur, meaning heart. A leader must have the heart to communicate his vision no matter how absurd it may sound to others, to risk defeat in the face of bitter odds, to put himself and his reputation on the line, and to reach out to others in order to take them on the journey. After all, a leader's courage is ultimately not for himself, but for all the people depending on him to lead.

Every significant relationship in your life
has your fingerprints all over it—
the fingerprints of your character. And those
impressions on another person's life are true indications
of what your character is really like.

—STEVE FARRAR

Leadership, like responsibility, is a voluntary act.

—JOHN C. MAXWELL

LEADERS THAT LAST . . .

develop personal discipline.

put their confidence in God.

keep the value of material possessions
in perspective.

recognize the danger of becoming
a slave to pleasure.

seek and refresh God's vision
for their lives.

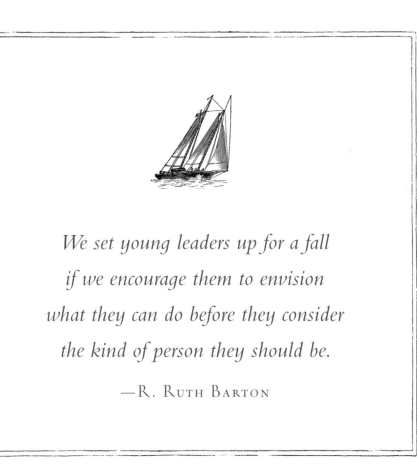

We set young leaders up for a fall
if we encourage them to envision
what they can do before they consider
the kind of person they should be.

—R. RUTH BARTON

Vision does not ignite growth; passion does.
Passion fuels vision and vision is the focus
of the power of passion. Leaders who are passionate
about their call create vision.

—KEN HEMPHILL

❖ ❖ ❖

God grant that men of principle
shall be our principal men.

—THOMAS JEFFERSON

The mark of the immature man is that he wants to die nobly for a cause, while the mark of a mature man is that he wants to live humbly for one.

—WILHELM STEKEL

Vision:

The Indispensable Quality of Leadership

All effective leaders have a vision of what they must accomplish. That vision becomes the energy behind every effort and the force that pushes through all the problems. With vision, a leader is on a mission. His or her contagious spirit is felt among the crowd until others begin to rise alongside.

One of the most common questions from people in leadership positions is, "How do I get a vision for my organization?" That is a crucial question, because until it is answered, a person will be a leader in name only.

Although I cannot give you a vision, I can share the process for finding one:

Look Within You—What Do You Feel?

You can't borrow somebody else's vision. It must come from inside of you. The thing that brings it out is passion.

Look Behind You—What Have You Learned?

Every leader's vision is based on his or her own personal experience. What does your past tell you about your future?

Look Around You—What Is Happening to Others?

As a leader, you must always take into account other people. If others aren't with you, you aren't leading.

Look Ahead of You—What Is the Big Picture?

Leaders don't get bogged down in the minutia. They see everything from the vantagepoint of the mountaintop. That's why their goals are called vision.

Look Above You—What Does God Expect of You?

No vision is worthy of your life unless it fulfills your destiny, the purpose for which you were designed. Your vision must contribute to your destiny.

Look Beside You—
What Resources Are Available to You?

Your vision must be bigger than you. The greater it is, the more resources it will require. The best leaders bring all of the resources in their world into play to accomplish something great.

Adapted from *Developing the Leader Within You*

You may have to fight a battle more than once to win it.

—Margaret Thatcher

❖ ❖ ❖

None but men of strong passions are capable of rising up to greatness.

—Honoré Gabriel Riqueti, comte de Maribeau

SECTION THREE

SACRIFICE

He who is required by the necessity of his position

to speak the highest things is compelled by the same

necessity to exemplify the highest things.

—GREGORY THE GREAT
(450–604)

45

I am only one, but still I am one.

I cannot do everything, but still I can do something;

And because I cannot do everything

I will not refuse to do the something that I can do.

—EDWARD EVERETT HALE

❖ ❖ ❖

The true measure of your character is

what you would do if you were sure

no one would ever find out.

—JOHN C. MAXWELL

GIVE UP *to* GO UP

One of the reasons leaders need courage and character is that sacrifice is often a crucial part of leadership. Take a look at these leaders from Scripture and what they gave up.

Noah: He was the first person to make great sacrifices to become a leader. How would you feel if you were required to give up every place and every person you had ever known (other than seven family members) to be the leader God wanted you to be? That's what Noah did. The world started over from scratch with him. Many people faced with the same prospect would have said, "Forget it," and lain down to die.

Abraham: The calling of Abraham involved his leaving his family and home in Ur to go to a land he'd never seen. He went not knowing where he was going. And after he got to his destination, he wasn't allowed to put down roots and establish himself. He lived in tents all his life.

Joseph: One of the most gifted and promising leaders in the history of the Hebrews was sold into slavery. He gave up his comfort, his home, and his freedom. Only after years of service and imprisonment was he freed from prison for interpreting Pharaoh's dreams. His reward was being put in charge of the most powerful nation on earth.

Nehemiah: This leader gave up a cushy job in the palace of a king to travel a thousand miles to a brokendown city in the boondocks. And when he got there, he faced opposition and death threats. Yet he was able to rebuild the city walls of Jerusalem, bringing pride and protection to its people.

Paul: This disciple of Jesus Christ gave up his secure life as a Pharisee of Pharisees to become an itinerant worker in Asia. Through the course of his career, he was persecuted, beaten, whipped, stoned, shipwrecked, and ultimately executed because of his leadership for the cause of Christ. He is considered the greatest of the apostles.

From *The 21 Most Powerful Minutes in a Leader's Day*

A life isn't significant except for

its impact on other lives.

—Jackie Robinson

Commitment in the face of conflict

creates character.

—John C. Maxwell

GLORY IN SACRIFICE

In 1945, in a Japanese internment camp in China, a forty-three-year-old man did everything he could to effectively lead and serve his fellow prisoners. Without the benefit of equipment or supplies, he taught science to many of the children in the makeshift school they created. He also taught Sunday school, led Bible studies for adults, and tended to the elderly and infirm.

Along with teaching and assisting others, he organized youth sporting events to promote fitness and boost morale. In fact, he especially enjoyed helping the children with athletics because he had been an athlete himself—an especially well-known one in England and his native Scotland. Many years earlier, the people had called him the "Flying Scotsman" because of his prowess in track.

If you've seen the movie *Chariots of Fire*, then you know his name: Eric Liddell. A 100-meter sprinter by talent and training, he declined to run in that race during the Paris Olympics of 1924 when he learned that it would be run on a Sunday. A devout Christian, he believed that running on Sunday violated the keeping of the Sabbath, something he would not do for king, country, or Olympic glory. For the stand he took, Eric Liddell was called a traitor.

True Account

The movie that tells his story and that of several other British athletes was remarkably accurate. For example, it portrayed Liddell competing in a race in which he was bumped off of the track. An actual account of the race from *The Student* (October 22, 1924) explained:

> *For a moment [Liddell] seemed half inclined to give up. Then suddenly he sprang forward and was after his opponents in a flash. By this time the leaders were twenty yards ahead, but Liddell gradually drew up on them, and by the time the home straight was reached he was running fourth. He would be about ten yards behind Gillis [the runner who had bumped him] then. It seemed out of the question that he would win, but he achieved the apparently impossible. Forty yards from home he was third and seemed on the point of collapsing, but pulling himself together he put in a desperate finish to win by two yards from Gillis.*

Not surprisingly, at the 1924 Olympics, Liddell performed in similar fashion. When he refused to run in the 100 meters, he instead got the opportunity to run in a 400-meters race. Though he had not trained for that distance, he took the opportunity. Remarkably, he not only won—he set a world record in the process!

The Call of Fame

The welcome that Liddell received in England was incredible, but it was nothing compared to the celebration in his native Scotland. What was his response to his fame? He quietly finished his degree in science and divinity, and then in 1925, he traveled to China as a missionary.

For nearly twenty years, he worked with the Chinese people, teaching, sharing his faith, and serving in numerous other ways. At one point, he worked with the Red Cross to gain greater access to more remote regions of the country. And he made the most of it.

While working with the Red Cross following the Japanese invasion of China, he once heard that a Chinese man lay wounded in a temple, the locals afraid to help him because they feared the violent reprisals of the Japanese military. Liddell traveled two days to find the man, who, Liddell found out, had suffered a botched beheading from a Japanese executioner. The man was rescued, the gash that stretched from the back of his head to his mouth was stitched up, and he recovered.

War Prisoner

In 1943, Eric Liddell found himself in a 150-by-200-yard internment camp along with eighteen hundred other "enemy nationals." While there, he served everyone he could, and the children there especially delighted in him. They had grown up hearing the story of the athlete who refused to run on Sunday. He gained not only the love of the children, but also that of the imprisoned adults and the respect and admiration of their Japanese captors.

A Calling Fulfilled

If Liddell was in great pain in early 1945, he never really let on. Despite his illness, he simply continued his responsibilities, teaching and coaching the children. But on February 21, 1945, just months before the end of the war, he succumbed to an undetected brain tumor. He was laid to rest in a little cemetery outside the walls of the camp.

The record books may remember Eric Liddell the runner, but the people whose lives he touched remember Eric Liddell the leader. In the end, where you lead and who you lead are less important than how you lead. The last few years of his life, Eric Liddell served mostly children.

He was someone who served wherever he was able, always offered a kind smile, and led by example. The race of the Christian life—not the Olympics—was the one that mattered most to him.

Being the first to cross the finish line

makes you a winner in only one phase of life.

It's what you do after you cross the line

that really counts.

—RALPH BOSTON,
OLYMPIC GOLD MEDALIST

THE PRINCE,
THEN THE PAUPER

The Dreamworks movie *The Prince of Egypt* captured the early life of Moses well. He grew up as a son of Pharaoh, a prince. As a boy, he enjoyed every pleasure of the palace, and he received the best of what Egypt offered physically and intellectually. Scripture explains, "Moses was learned in all the wisdom of the Egyptians, and was mighty in words and deeds" (Acts 7:22).

Yet Moses was willing to risk losing all of that to try to help his fellow Hebrews. After rashly murdering an Egyptian who was beating another Hebrew, he endured a forty-year exile in the desert of Midian. He went from privilege to poverty, from the world's capital to the wilderness, from adopted son to obscure shepherd.

When Moses fled Egypt, he probably thought he had risked and lost everything for nothing, but after forty years, Moses had undergone the breaking and remaking process required for him to be used by God. He had gone from an arrogant child of privilege who thought he could deliver the Hebrews single-handedly, to a man of God who was very humble, more than anyone else on the face of the earth.

Leadership always has a cost. To be a leader, you may not be asked to leave your country or give up all your possessions, as Moses was. But you can be sure that leading others will have a price.

From *The 21 Most Powerful Minutes in a Leader's Day*

Self-preservation is the first law of nature;
self-sacrifice the highest rule of grace.

—Author Unknown

In this world, it is not what we take up,
but what we give up, that makes us rich.

—Henry Ward Beecher

In Germany the Nazis came first for the Communists, and I didn't speak up because I wasn't a Communist. Then they came for the Jews, and I didn't speak up because I wasn't a Jew. Then they came for the trade unionists, and I didn't speak up because I wasn't a trade unionist. Then they came for the Catholics, and I didn't speak up because I was a Protestant. Then they came for me—and by that time no one was left to speak up.

—MARTIN NIEMÖLLER

SECTION FOUR

RISK

❖

It is not because things are difficult
that we do not dare; it is because
we do not dare that they are difficult.

—SENECA

AN
UNLIKELY
LEADER

She wasn't a very impressive looking woman—just a little over five feet tall, in her late thirties, with dark-brown weathered skin. She couldn't read or write. The clothes she wore were coarse and worn, though neat. When she smiled, people could see that her top two front teeth were missing.

She lived alone. It was said that she had abandoned her husband when she was twenty-nine. She gave him no warning. One day he woke up, and she was gone. She talked to him only once after that, years later, and she never mentioned his name again afterward.

Her employment was intermittent. Most of the time she took domestic jobs in small hotels: scrubbing floors, making up rooms, and cooking. But just about every spring and fall, she would disappear from her place of employment, come back broke, and work again to scrape together what little money she could. When she was present on the job, she worked hard and seemed physically tough, but she also was known to have fits where she would suddenly fall asleep. She attributed her affliction to a blow to the head she had taken during a teenage fight.

Who would respect a woman like this? The answer is the hundreds of slaves who followed her to freedom out of the South—they recognized and respected her leadership. So did just about every abolitionist in New England. The year was 1857. The woman's name was Harriet Tubman.

A Leader By Any Other Name

While she was only in her thirties, Harriet Tubman came to be called
"Moses" because of her ability to go into the land of captivity and bring
so many of her people out of slavery's bondage. Tubman started life as
a slave herself. She was born in 1820 and grew up in the farmland of
Maryland. When she was thirteen, she received the blow to her head
that troubled her all her life. She was in a store, and a white overseer
demanded her assistance so that he could beat an escaping slave. When
she refused and blocked the overseer's way, the man threw a two-pound
weight that hit Tubman in the head. She nearly died.

At age twenty-four, she married John Tubman, a free black man.
But when she talked to him about escaping to freedom in the North, he
wouldn't hear of it. He said that if she tried to leave, he'd turn her in. So
when she resolved to take her chances and go north in 1849, she did so
alone, without a word to him. Her first biographer, Sarah Bradford, said
that Tubman told her:

> I had reasoned this out in my mind: there was one of two things I had a
> right to, liberty or death. If I could not have one, I would have the other,
> for no man should take me alive. I should fight for my liberty as my

strength lasted, and when the time came for me to go, the Lord would let them take me.[6]

Tubman made her way to Philadelphia, Pennsylvania, via the Underground Railroad, a secret network of free blacks, white abolitionists, and Quakers who helped escaping slaves on the run. Though free herself, she vowed to return to Maryland and bring her family out. In 1850, she made her first return trip as an Underground Railroad "conductor"—someone who retrieved and guided slaves out with the assistance of sympathizers along the way.

A Leader of Steel

Each summer and winter, Tubman worked for the funds she needed to make return trips to the South. And every spring and fall, she risked her life by going south and returning with more people. She was fearless. And her leadership was unshakable. It was extremely dangerous work, and when people in her charge wavered, she was strong as steel, knowing that escaped slaves who failed would be beaten and tortured until they gave information about those who had helped them. So she never allowed any people she was guiding to give up. "Dead folks tell no tales," she would tell a faint-hearted slave as she put a loaded pistol to his head. "You go on or die!"

Between 1850 and 1860, Harriet Tubman guided out more than three hundred people, including many of her own family members. She made nineteen trips in all and was very proud of the fact that she never once lost a single person under her care. "I never ran my train off the track," she once said, "and I never lost a passenger." Southern whites put a $12,000 price on her head—a fortune at that time. Southern blacks simply called her Moses. By the start of the Civil War, she had brought more people out of slavery than any other American in history—black or white, male or female.

Increasing Respect

Tubman's reputation and influence commanded respect, and not just among slaves who dreamed of gaining their freedom. Influential northerners of both races sought her out, such as Senator William Seward, who later became Abraham Lincoln's Secretary of State, and outspoken abolitionist and former slave Frederick Douglas. Tubman's advice and leadership were also requested by John Brown, the famed revolutionary abolitionist. Brown always referred to the former slave as "General

Tubman," and was quoted as saying she "was a better officer than most whom he had seen, and could command an army as successfully as she had led her small parties of fugitives."

A Test Of Leadership

Harriet Tubman would appear to be an unlikely candidate for leadership, because the deck was certainly stacked against her. She was uneducated. She lived in a culture that didn't respect African Americans. And she labored in a country where women didn't even have the right to vote yet. Despite her circumstances, she became an incredible leader.

From *The 21 Irrefutable Laws of Leadership*

Greatness, in the last analysis,
is largely due to bravery—courage in
escaping from old ideas and old standards
and respectable ways of doing things.

—JAMES HARVEY ROBINSON

⊸∞⊶

I'd rather give my life
than be afraid to give it.

—LYNDON B. JOHNSON

MARCHING OFF THE MAP

Leaders take risks. That's not to say that they are reckless, because good leaders aren't. But they don't always take the safest route. Rarely can a person break ground and play it safe at the same time. Often, leaders must take others into the unknown, and march them off the map.

Look at wise leaders who take risks, and you will find that they:

Gather information wisely.

Risk from strength.

Prepare thoroughly.

Fail successfully.

Display flexibility.

Observe timing.

Envision what can be gained.

Understand what is at stake.

Stay on mission.

Possess the right motives.

Give their followers wins.

March forward with confidence.

The Fire to Fuel a Regiment

A nineteenth century circuit-riding preacher named Peter Cartwright was preparing to deliver a sermon one Sunday when he was warned that President Andrew Jackson was in attendance and was asked to keep his remarks inoffensive. During that message, he included this statement: "I have been told that Andrew Jackson is in this congregation. And I have been asked to guard my remarks. What I must say is that Andrew Jackson will go to hell if he doesn't repent of his sin."

After the sermon, Jackson strode up to Cartwright. "Sir," the President said, "if I had a regiment of men like you, I could whip the world."

From *The 21 Indispensable Qualities of a Leader*

Virtue is bold, and goodness never fearful.

—William Shakespeare

CHANCE
OF A LIFETIME

One morning in late July of 1940, Japanese Consul-General Chiune Sugihara awakened to find a throng of Jewish refugees outside the gate of the Japanese consulate in Kaunas, Lithuania. Most of them had fled from Poland, barely escaping the grasp of the Nazis during their invasion of that country. But once again, with the Nazis advancing, they were trapped.

On that morning, they were seeking the help of Sugihara because word had spread among them that there was still one way out of Lithuania: They could travel through the Soviet Union, into Japan, and on to freedom in the Caribbean. The only thing they lacked were transit visas from the Japanese government.

Sugihara, a forty-year-old diplomat with a promising career, immediately wired Tokyo to obtain permission to write the visas, but his government refused to grant it. He wired them again, and again they refused. He tried a third time and was not only refused, but told to stop inquiring.

Sugihara faced a dilemma. On the one hand, he was a faithful Japanese, taught from birth to respect and obey authority. If he disregarded his orders, his family would probably be disgraced, and their lives would be in jeopardy. On the other hand, he was from a samurai family, taught to help people in need. Further, he was also a Christian, having converted as a young man.

His choice was clear. For the next twenty-nine days, he and his wife, Yukiko, spent every moment writing transit visas. Normally, a consul might write three hundred visas in a month. Sugihara wrote more

SECTION FIVE

DETERMINATION

✦

There is no royal road to anything. One thing at a time, all things in succession. That which grows fast withers as rapidly; that which grows slowly endures.

—JOSIAH G. HOLLAND

Your character is your most
effective means of persuasion.

—John C. Maxwell

Some men succeed by what they know;
some by what they do; and a few
by what they are.

—Elbert Hubbard

WHEN DO LEADERS NEED DETERMINATION?

When they *seek* the truth.

When they *desire* to change.

When they *express* their convictions.

When they *want* to overcome obstacles.

When they *wish* to learn and grow.

When they *seek* to take the high road.

When they *lead!*

THE
ACE OF ACES

Why do these three men have in common: the auto racer who set the world speed record at Daytona in 1914, the pilot who recorded the highest number of victories in aerial combat against the Germans in World War I, and the Secretary of War's special advisor who survived a plane crash and twenty-two days on a raft in the Pacific during World War II?

They all lived through dangerous circumstances. They all displayed courage and steely nerves under duress. And they all happen to be the same person—Eddie Rickenbacker.

Meeting a challenge was never a big problem for Eddie Rickenbacker, whether it was physical, mental, or economic. When he was twelve, his father died, and he quit school to become the family's primary breadwinner. He sold newspapers, eggs, and goat's milk. He worked in a glass factory, brewery, shoe factory, and foundry. Then as a teenager, he started working as a race car mechanic, and at age twenty-two, he began racing. Two years later he set the world speed record.

When the United States entered World War I, Rickenbacker tried to enlist as an aviator, but he was overage and undereducated. So instead he entered as a chauffeur and then talked his superiors into sending him to flight training. Despite not fitting in with his college educated fellow aviators, he excelled as a pilot. And by the time the war was over, he had logged 300 combat hours (the most of any American pilot), survived 134 aerial encounters with the enemy, claimed 26 kills, and earned the Medal of Honor, 8 Distinguished Service Crosses, and the French Legion of Honor. He was also promoted to captain and put in command of his squadron.

Rickenbacker's prowess in the air caused the press to dub him the "American Ace of Aces." When asked about his courage in combat, he admitted that he had been afraid. "Courage," he said, "is doing what you're afraid to do. There can be no courage unless you're scared."

That courage served the Ace of Aces well after World War I. In 1933, he became the vice-president of Eastern Air Transport (later Eastern Airlines). Back then all airlines existed only because they were subsidized by the government. But Rickenbacker thought they should be self-sufficient. He decided to completely change the way the company did business. Within two years he made Eastern profitable, a first in aviation history. And when the President of the United States canceled all commercial carriers' air mail contracts, Rickenbacker took him on—and won. Rickenbacker led Eastern successfully for thirty years and retired at age seventy-three. When he died ten years later, his son, William, wrote, "If he had a motto, it must have been the phrase I've heard a thousand times: 'I'll fight like a wildcat!'"

From *The 21 Indispensable Qualities of a Leader*

Leaders are pioneers. They are people who venture into unexplored territory. They guide us to new and often unfamiliar destinations. People who take the lead are foot soldiers in the campaigns for change. . . the unique reason for having leaders—their differentiating function—is to move us forward. Leaders get us going someplace.

—JAMES M. KOUZES & BARRY Z. POSNER

It is wisdom to use your influence. . . It is criminal to sell it.

—ED COLE

Good character is more to be praised than outstanding talent. Most talents are, to some extent, a gift. Good character, by contrast, is not given to us. We have to build it piece by piece— by thought, choice, courage, and determination.

—JOHN LUTHER

We don't need more strength or more ability or greater opportunity. What we need to use is what we have.

—BASIL WALSH

How Do You Become an Influencer With the Right to Lead?

Have Integrity with Others

Nurture Others

Have Faith in Others

Listen to Others

Understand Others

Enlarge Others

Navigate for Others

Connect with Others

Empower Others

Produce Other Influencers

LOVE LETTERS

Every true student of the game of basketball knows John Wooden. His resume is filled with unbroken records and reads like no one else's:

—Ten NCAA championships

—An eighty-eight game winning streak that lasted from January 30, 1971 to January 17, 1974

—Four undefeated seasons

—Only one losing season in his forty-year career (his first year—as a high school coach)

—First person inducted into the Hall of Fame as both player and coach

Wooden is known as a man of meticulous detail (each season he taught players the right way to put on their socks), total team participation (the equipment manager was respected and valued as much as a starting player), and uncompromising dedication to excellence (his staff spent two hours each day planning practices that often didn't last two hours). No leader in sports is more solid than John Wooden.

What most people may not know is that John Wooden is just as steady and true in quiet retirement as he was in the noisy spotlight of college sports. Rick Reilly, of Sports Illustrated, describes Wooden as "quiet as an April snow and square as a game of checkers; loyal to one woman, one school, one way."[7]

True to Wooden's nature, on the twenty-first of each month he sits down and writes a love letter to Nellie, his wife of fifty-three years. Once he's shared his heart with her, he carefully puts the letter in an envelope and places it with the others in their bedroom, all neatly tied with a yellow ribbon. So far, there are more than 180 of those love letters. And they remain unopened. You see, it's been fifteen years since his beloved Nellie died.

Not a month has passed that Wooden hasn't written to her. "I'm not afraid to die," Wooden has said. "Death is my only chance to be with her again." I suspect that the first time he misses writing one of those letters, it will be because he is delivering the message to her face-to-face.

John Wooden was a man of hall-of-fame character long before he was a hall-of-fame coach.

The harder you work,
the harder it is to surrender.

—Vince Lombardi

❧

If you aren't going all the way,
why go at all?

—Joe Namath

SECTION SIX

SERVICE

❖

You've got to love your people

more than your position.

—John C. Maxwell

Leadership must be based on goodwill. Goodwill does not mean posturing and, least of all, pandering to the mob. It means obvious and wholehearted commitment to helping followers. We are tired of leaders we fear, tired of leaders we love, and most tired of leaders who let us take liberties with them. What we need for leaders are men of the heart who are so helpful that they, in effect, do away with the need of their jobs. But leaders like that are never out of a job, never out of followers. Strange as it sounds, great leaders gain authority by giving it away.

—ADMIRAL JAMES B. STOCKDALE

The purpose of life is not to win. The purpose of life is to grow and to share. When you come to look back on all that you have done in life, you will get more satisfaction from the pleasure you have brought into other people's lives than you will from the times that you outdid and defeated them.

—Rabbi Harold Kushner

True heroism is remarkably sober, very undramatic. It is not the urge to surpass all others at whatever the cost, but the urge to serve others at whatever cost.

—Arthur Ashe

A FARMER
ANSWERS THE CALL

On June 15, 1775, the eve of the American Revolution, John Adams rose from his seat in Congress and made his nomination for the appointment of General and Commander in Chief of the United Colonies. His fellow statesmen quickly confirmed his nomination. Who did they appoint to this position that would likely determine the outcome of the American revolution against Great Britain? The answer is George Washington.

Why would the founding fathers of our country choose Washington, a forty-three-year-old gentleman farmer from Virginia, as the man to face experienced British generals such as Sir William Howe, Sir Henry Clinton, and Charles Lord Cornwallis, and as the man who would one day become Governor-General of India?

First Action

Though born in 1732 into the family of a Virginia planter, young George was not content to stay on the farm. As a teenager, he learned surveying and traveled in the wilderness as far as the Shenandoah Valley as part of a surveying team for Lord Thomas Fairfax. A few years after that, Washington joined the Virginia militia and began studying the military arts.

In 1753, he was selected for an important mission. The French had entered the Ohio River Valley and were preparing to build a fort on land the British had claimed but not yet settled. An envoy would be needed to blaze a trail through the hostile wilderness, meet with the French commander, and deliver a message from the British Crown demanding that the rival group relinquish their claim and depart from the region. It was a difficult assignment requiring many qualities: skill and stamina to travel through rough wilderness, courage to face hostile Native Americans, and diplomatic ability to interact with the French. And though he was only twenty-one years old, Washington received the assignment. He completed it with great success, delivering the message to the French commander near modern-day Pittsburgh, and returning with his response in the dead of winter through the territory of Native Americans who tried to hunt him down and kill him.

Because of his success, in 1754 Washington was promoted to lieutenant colonel and selected to lead 160 soldiers back into the area to fight the French. A year later, he again returned to the Ohio River Valley as a volunteer aide de camp to General Edward Braddock. It was in the company of Braddock that Washington made his reputation as a brave and poised warrior under fire. When the British and colonial forces under Braddock's command were ambushed by French and Native American fighters in a ravine near the Monongahela River, Washington took action. He seemed to be everywhere at once: He charged to Braddock's side to help inspire the regular troops to fight their way out of the ambush. He rode to the rear to bring the Virginia militiamen up into the fight. And as officer after officer was killed or wounded (including Braddock), Washington rallied and directed the troops. He is credited with saving the men who finally did escape.

In all, sixty officers were killed. During the battle, Washington himself had two horses shot from under him and discovered after the fighting that four bullets had ripped through his coat. It was reported that so many Native Americans had tried to kill him—and failed—that they finally gave up, believing that he was under the special protection of the "great spirit."

Regimental Commander

A month later, Washington found himself promoted to colonel and became the regimental commander over all Virginia forces. He was only twenty-three years old.

Though Washington wanted to make a career as a soldier, he was frustrated with the intermittent support of the governor, the poor pay, and the lack of respect given to colonial officers. When he was able to win election to the Virginia House of Burgesses in 1758, he resigned his commission, retired to Mount Vernon, and determined to serve through political rather than military leadership. For a decade and a half, he did serve. And he was also elected to the First and Second Continental Congresses, which led to his appointment as leader of the Continental Army in 1775.

Commander in Chief

Washington had earned the right to lead the army. And for six years, he masterfully commanded the troops, facing a superior enemy, enduring great hardship, and battling more experienced generals. But he managed to sustain the freedom of the United States, and in 1781, he defeated the British troops and forced the surrender of General Cornwallis.

Though Washington preserved the fledgling government through battle with Britain, he also faced serious problems at home. More than once people recommended to him that he make himself king of the country. And after Congress neglected to pay the officers of the army for a considerable period, in March of 1783 a group of them met at their headquarters in Newburgh, New York, to discuss the action they might take against the government. The majority suggested that Washington seize power using the army to back himself.

Washington refused and then tried to persuade the soldiers to give their government leaders time to do the right thing. The officers were unmoved. In a final attempt to calm them, he decided he should read them a letter he had recently received from a congressman. Then, in one moment that altered the course of history, he paused, looked at the letter with difficulty, and finally reached into his pocket for his eyeglasses. Quietly he remarked, "I have already grown gray in the service of my country. I am now going blind." The comment stunned his officers, and it turned the tide of their opinion. Washington biographer James Flexner commented, "This was probably the most important single gathering ever held in the United States."

One More Service

A month later, to the great surprise of many, Washington resigned his commission as Commander of the Army. Why? Because when he took the position, he had promised he would resign when his job was done. Again he retired to Mount Vernon. But when the country needed to elect its first leader, someone who could guide them through those first precarious years, they looked again to Washington, a man who valued service rather than power. The Electoral College was unanimous in its choice of him as president, the only time in the nation's history. Of the many patriots and valiant leaders who had risen to liberate the people of the United States—and there were many—George Washington, more than any other, had earned the right to lead.

———— ⁕ ————

I love the man that can smile in trouble, that can gather strength from distress, and grow brave by reflection. 'Tis the business of little minds to shrink, but he whose heart is firm, and whose conscience approves his conduct, will pursue his principles unto death.

—Thomas Paine, Revolutionary Patriot

*Leaders provide for their people
what the people cannot provide for themselves.*

—JOHN C. MAXWELL

⸺⸺

*A leader is not an administrator who loves to
run others, but someone who carries water for
his people so they can get on with their jobs.*

—ROBERT TOWNSEND

I would be true for there are those who trust me;

I would be pure, for there are those who care;

I would be strong, for there is much to suffer;

I would be brave, for there is much to dare;

I would be friend of all—the poor, the friendless;

I would be giving and forget the gift;

I would be humble, for I know my weakness;

I would look up—and laugh, and love, and lift.

—Author Unknown

INTEGRITY

❖

If I take care of my character,
my reputation will take care of itself.

—DWIGHT L. MOODY

Character may be manifested in the great moments,
but it is made in the small ones.

—Phillips Brooks

Integrity is the rock upon which we build our
business success—our quality products and services,
our forthright relations with customers and suppliers,
and ultimately, our winning competitive record.
GE's quest for competitive excellence begins
and ends with our commitment to ethical conduct.

—Jack Welch, Chairman of General Electric
SPEAKING TO HIS EMPLOYEES

INTEGRITY FROM WISDOM

King Solomon of ancient Israel is said to have been the wisest man on earth. Though in the end he didn't finish well as a leader, he understood the importance of integrity and sought to live by it. In Proverbs he wrote, "He who walks with integrity walks securely, But he who perverts his ways will become known" (10:9 NKJV).

FEARLESS
TO A
FAULT

Not long ago, the movie *Gladiator* appeared in theaters. It told the story of a great Roman general named Maximus who served the emperor, Marcus Aurelius.

During the emperor's last days, he fought the barbarians to the north of the Roman Empire. But Maximus was betrayed by the emperor's son, Commodus, a spoiled cowardly politician lately arrived at the frontier. As a result of Commodus' treachery Emporer Aurelius died, his wicked son became emperor in his place, and Maximus narrowly escaped death only to be sold into slavery and forced to live as a gladiator. Though fictional, it is a gripping story of courage and resolve. But it's not as remarkable as the story of the real Commodus.

It's true that Commodus was Marcus Aurelius' son and heir. But unlike his fictional counterpart, he accompanied his father into battle for most of his early life. When his father died of plague, Commodus became emperor at age nineteen. He quickly made peace with the empire's enemies on the border and returned to Rome.

The new emperor entered the capitol as a hero, and he then tried to position himself as a man of the people. Much to the dismay of the ruling classes, Commodus soon began proving his courage and skill by performing in the Coliseum. He killed lions, rhinoceroses, and elephants. A skilled bowman, he felled numerous other animals with single shots with his bow. In one encounter, he killed one hundred leopards using one hundred javelins. It's said that the rapport Commodus gained with the common people was remarkable.

Commodus, unlike his movie counterpart, was a skilled warrior. Facing wild beasts eventually wasn't enough of a test for him. In time, he entered the arena with weapons of war and faced the finest gladiators in Rome. And he beat them all. He was truly a man of courage.

Though a brave and skilled warrior, Commodus' character was another matter. He spent much of his time trying to impress the people and proclaim his glory. He fancied himself the new "founder" of Rome, even going so far as to rename the empire after himself. He also thought of himself as a modern-day Hercules. He often wore animal skins and carried a club, much like the mythological figure was reputed to have done. He also changed the Roman calendar—renaming each of the months after one of the many titles he had given himself.

In time, the barbarians in the north continued to encroach on the Roman empire's borders, while Commodus lived in its capital and occupied himself with taxing the rich, distributing money to the poor, having senators and other political enemies executed, and reinventing himself.

The last straw for the Senate and the people came when

Commodus declared that he intended to accept the honor of being consul—the highest and most revered office in all of Rome—while dressed as a gladiator. The night before he was to accept the consulship, the people closest to him drugged him and then strangled him to death. He was thirty-one years old.

Commodus seemed to have everything—position, skill, courage, power, wealth. He had everything except a character of integrity. And that's the one thing a leader cannot do without.

Few things are more dangerous than a leader with an unexamined life.

—JOHN C. MAXWELL

In order to be a leader, a man must have followers. And to have followers, a man must have their confidence. Hence the supreme quality for a leader is unquestionably integrity. Without it, no real success is possible, no matter whether it is on a section gang, a football field, in an army, or in an office. If a man's associates find him guilty of phoniness, if they find that he lacks forthright integrity, he will fail. His teachings and actions must square with each other. The first great need, therefore, is integrity and high purpose.

—Dwight D. Eisenhower

As a leader, you have to take responsibility for your own failures as well as successes. That's the only way you'll learn. If you keep learning, you'll improve. If you improve, your leadership will get better. And in time, you will earn the right to lead on the level you deserve.

—JOHN C. MAXWELL

❧

Men will never cast away their dearest pleasures upon the drowsy request of someone who does not even seem to mean what he says.

—RICHARD BAXTER

THE GUY IN THE GLASS

When you get what you want in your struggle for pelf,
And the world makes you King for a day,
Then go to the mirror and look at yourself,
And see what that guy has to say.

For it isn't your Father, or Mother, or Wife,
Who judgement upon you must pass.
The feller whose verdict counts most in your life
Is the guy staring back from the glass.

He's the feller to please, never mind all the rest,
For he's with you clear up to the end,
And you've passed your most dangerous, difficult test
If the guy in the glass is your friend.

You may be like Jack Horner and "chisel" a plum,

And think you're a wonderful guy,

But the man in the glass says you're only a bum

If you can't look him straight in the eye.

You can fool the whole world down the pathway of years,

And get pats on the back as you pass,

But your final reward will be heartaches and tears

If you cheated the guy in the glass.

—Dale Wimbrow

Ask a bunch of experts what it takes to be a leader, and you'll hear a lot of answers. "Vision," one will say. "Knowledge," another will tell you. "Communication, problem solving, people skills." All good answers. Look at a great leader, and you will find all of those qualities. But no matter how many positive qualities a leader possesses, he cannot lead for long if he lacks character. Without character, even the most talented leader's contribution to his followers will be far short-reaching, shallower than its potential, and easily forgotten.

Of those to whom much is given, much is required.
And when at some future date the high court of history
sits in judgment on each of us—recording
whether in our brief span of service we fulfilled
our responsibilities—our success or failure,
we will be measured by the answers to four questions—
were we truly men of courage . . .
were we truly men of judgment . . .
were we truly men of integrity . . .
were we truly men of dedication?

—JOHN F. KENNEDY

*I hope I shall always possess firmness
and virtue enough to maintain, what I
consider the most enviable of all titles,
the character of an honest man.*

—GEORGE WASHINGTON

THE VALUE OF INTEGRITY

Integrity will take a leader farther
than any other single quality:

⚬⚬⚬

Integrity is more than our talk.

Integrity brings security.

Integrity's absence leads to ruin.

⚬⚬⚬

If you would travel far and
do much as a leader, never compromise
your integrity.

Since you have appointed the blind guide

to lead them, for their sakes,

Lord, if not for mine, teach him whom

you have made to be their teacher;

lead him whom you have bidden

to lead them; rule him who is their ruler.

—AELRED,
ABBOT OF RIEVAULX (1109–1167)

We are blind until we see
That in the human plan
Nothing is worth the making
If it does not make the man.

Why build these cities glorious
If man unbuilded goes?
In vain we build the world
Unless the builder grows.

—EDWIN MARKHAM

About the Author

John C. Maxwell is an internationally recognized leadership expert, speaker, and author who has sold over 18 million books. His organizations have trained more than 2 million leaders worldwide. Dr. Maxwell is the founder of EQUIP and INJOY Stewardship Services. Every year he speaks to Fortune 500 companies, international government leaders, and audiences as diverse as the United States Military Academy at West Point, the National Football League, and ambassadors at the United Nations. A *New York Times, Wall Street Journal*, and *Business Week* best-selling author, Maxwell was named the World's Top Leadership Guru by Leadershipgurus.net. He was also one of only 25 authors and artists named to Amazon.com's 10th Anniversary Hall of Fame. Three of his books, *The 21 Irrefutable Laws of Leadership, Developing the Leader Within You*, and *The 21 Indispensable Qualities of a Leader* have each sold over a million copies.

MARE BALEARIDES

INSULAE

INS. MINORCA

c. Bajoles
S. Catherine
Fornelle
Citadella
Alcor
Maon
Port de Maon
Laire de Maon

Puglionza
MALI-OR
Palomera
CA
Alcudia
Mallorca
INS
C. de la Pera
Catalunga
BALE
Torre Colombo
Cap
ARICUM
Stor
Dragonera
Porto Pedre
Figuer

c. de Tagomago
Cubrera Ins.

PYTYVSAE
INSVLAE
ormentera t
en el
inla

ITERRANEI

ITERR

Z. de
Gargal

Acknowldgements

Grateful acknowldgement is made to the following for permission to reprint copyrighted material.

John C. Maxwell. 1993.
Developing the Leader Within You.
Nashville, TN: Thomas Nelson Publishers.

John C. Maxwell. 1998.
The 21 Irrefutable Laws of Leadership:
Follow Them and People Will Follow You.
Nashville, TN: Thomas Nelson Publishers.

John C. Maxwell. 1999.
The 21 Indispensable Qualities of a Leader: Becoming the Person Others Will
Want to Follow.
Nashville, TN: Thomas Nelson Publishers.

John C. Maxwell. 2000.
The 21 Most Powerful Minutes in a
Leader's Day: Revitalize Your Spirit and Empower Your Leadership.
Nashville, TN: Thomas Nelson Publishers.

Peter Dale Wimbrow. 1934.
"The Guy in the Glass."

Notes

1. Schwarzkopf, Norman H. 1992.
   It Doesn't Take a Hero.
   New York City, NY: Bantam Books, Inc.

2. Personal letter from Kent Millard.

3. Mandela, Nelson. 1995.
   Long Walk to Freedom.
   Boston, MA: Little, Brown and Company.

4. Mandela, Nelson.
   "An Autobiographical Note by Nelson Mandela, 1964."
   From the African National Congress Web site:
   http://www.anc.org.za/ancdocs/history/mandela/auto.html

5. Brink, Andre, "Mandela." Time. April 13, 1998, p. 190.

6. Bradford, Sarah H. 1993.
   Harriet Tubman: The Moses of Her People.
   Applewood Books.

7. Reilly, Rick.
   "A Paragon Rising above the Madness."
   Sports Illustrated. March 30, 2000.

Copyright© 2009 Simple Truths, LLC

Published by SimpleTruths, LLC
1952 McDowell Road, Suite 205
Naperville, Illinois 60563
800-900-3427
www.simpletruths.com

This edition published under license from Simple Truths, LLC
exclusively for Thomas Nelson, Inc.

Design and production: Jared McDaniel, Studio430.com

All photos provided by Shutterstock.com

ISBN 978-1-4041-8942-3

2 3 4 5 RRD 13 12 11 10

Printed in China

www.thomasnelson.com